Mountains

Mountains

Seb Doubinsky

LEAKY BOOT PRESS

Mountains
by Seb Doubinsky

First published in 2017 by
Leaky Boot Press
http://www.leakyboot.com

Copyright © 2017 Seb Doubinsky
All rights reserved

No part of this book may be reproduced or transmitted in any form or by any means, electronic, mechanical, photocopying, recording, or otherwise, without prior written permission of the author.

ISBN: 978-1-909849-42-6

Mountains

"O poet!
can you write poetry
with sand in your ass?"
"Yes, of course
but it takes discipline"

Mountains

what will silence say when we are gone?
who will silence be?
a stone a river a cloud
or a bird between a branch
and the grass?

the scream that bounces back at you
from the side of the mountain
is not yours anymore
it is the mountain's and it tells you
it is accepting your gift

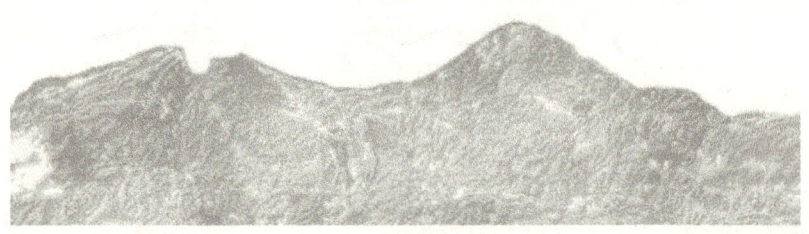

Mountains

the fish-hook of the moon
a cloud swims by
no catch this time

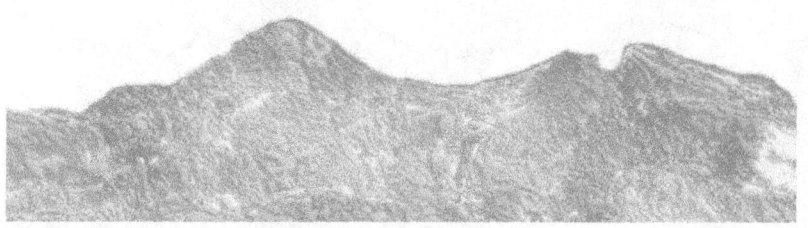

the flatness of this poem
like the flatness of the earth
is either a wish or an illusion

Mountains

a night as warm as a blanket
the old spire sweats copper
and lovers push the sheets aside
wishing the stars were ice-cubes
they could rub on their skin

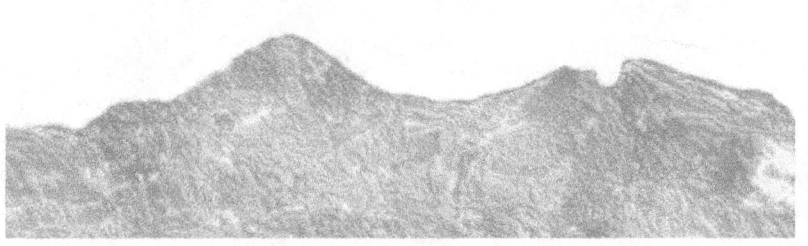

the generosity of poetry
like of nature
is always purely accidental

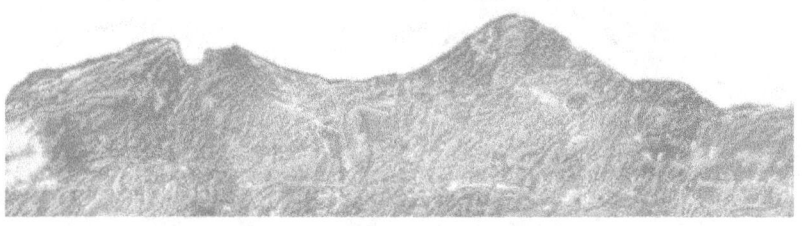

Mountains

if the wind can bend a river
I wonder what it can do
to our souls

(to Marly Youmans)

behind my eyelids
lies a dark country
full of ghosts

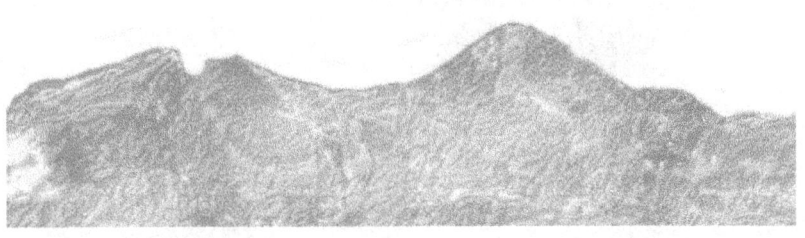

Mountains

clouds in the sky
like still arrows
aimed at the sun
birds in the sky
like small black stones
thrown at my heart

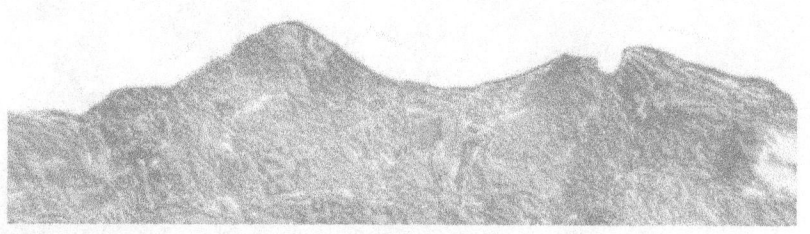

the terrifying power of nature
is only a reminder of our own
but nature is blind and we are not

Mountains

expertise has replaced
good old knowledge
these days and we wonder
why our empires crumble
three new flowers
have sprouted
in the garden
one yellow
one red
and one blue

the poet smokes
on top of the mountain
small cloud large clouds

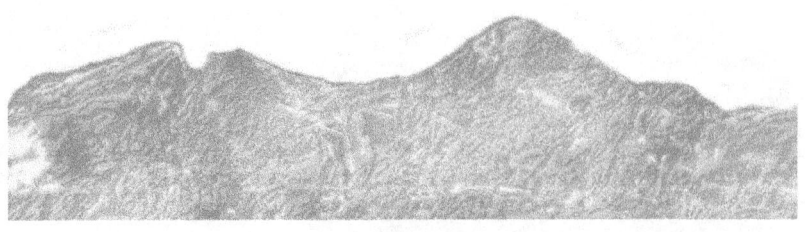

Mountains

smell of cut grass and gasoline
buzz of the lawnmower in the neighbor's garden
the poet waits for summer and turns a page of his book

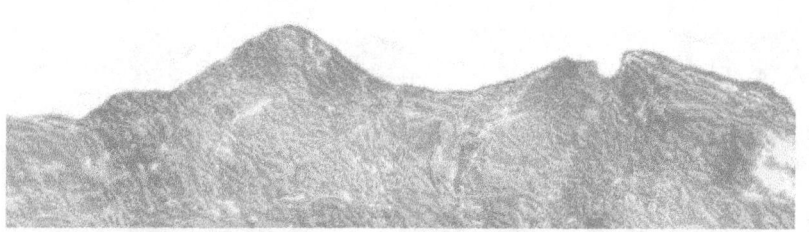

rain and sun
a few clouds
the poet hurries to work
arguing with the wind

the cars slumber under the rain
heavy beasts of gasoline burden
a bird hops by
unburdened tiny soul of feathers

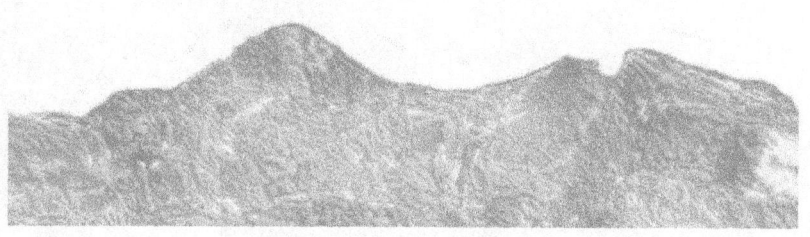

Seb Doubinsky

the sky is at peace
the earth is at peace
the poet smokes a cigarette
his lungs are working hard
but his mind is at peace

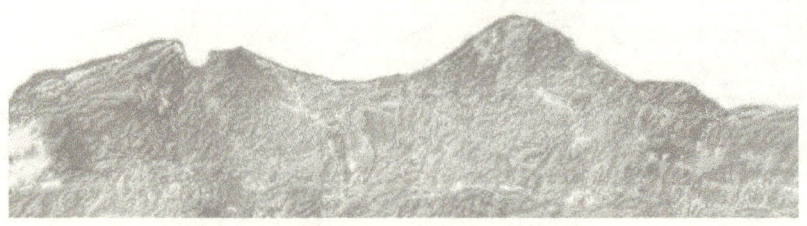

Mountains

nature mumbles something
into the poet's ear
thunder on the mountain

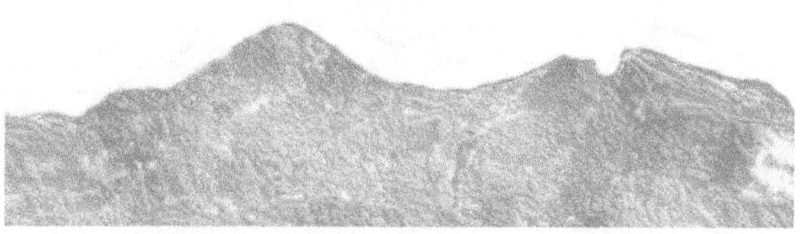

like poetry clouds change shape endlessly and disappear
to reappear further away - the poet lights another cigarette
and thinks about what he will have for dinner

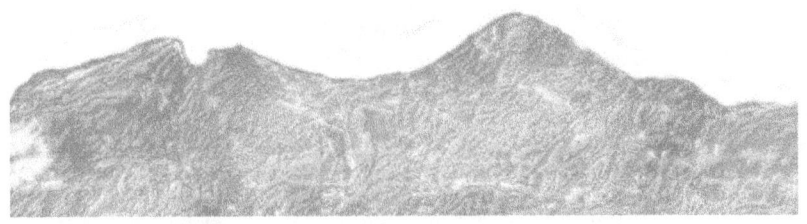

Mountains

rain falls
the cat yawns
the poet yawns too

the sun draws shapes on the roofs
the wind competes with the birds
the kids laugh downstairs
summer knocks at my door
hello hello welcome in

Mountains

the poet visits his friend the painter
the sun plays on the wall
they both see a different image

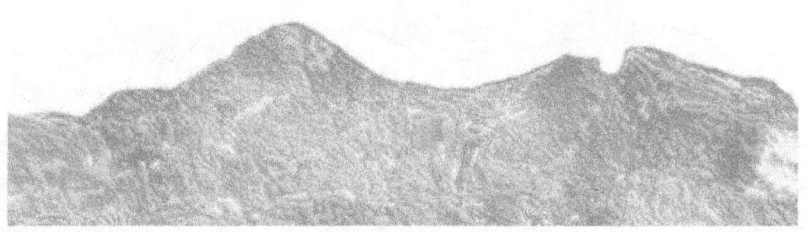

no warm sun warming
no fresh wind freshing
no new poem newing

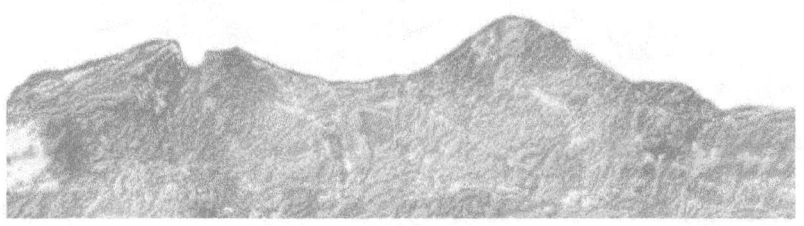

Mountains

the city turns its back to the clouds
they decide to go to the beach instead
the poet cycles faster on his way home

the path is long
the mountain steep
the poet's old sandals are perfect

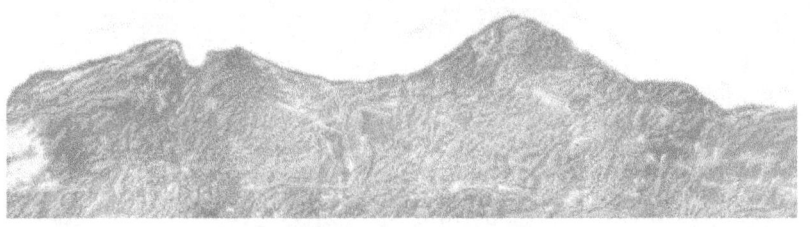

Mountains

scenes and scenes of poetry
the trip is endless but somewhat distracting
the poet wonders what he has forgotten at home

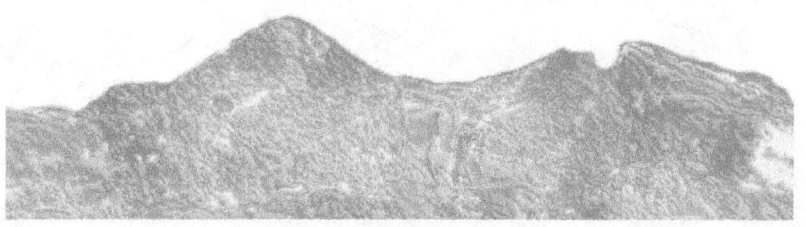

walking on the mountain path
the poet thinks of his hometown
but he doesn't miss it a bit
a butterfly flies past
and he has already forgotten it

Mountains

rain on the mountain
rain on the sea
the cat licks its paw

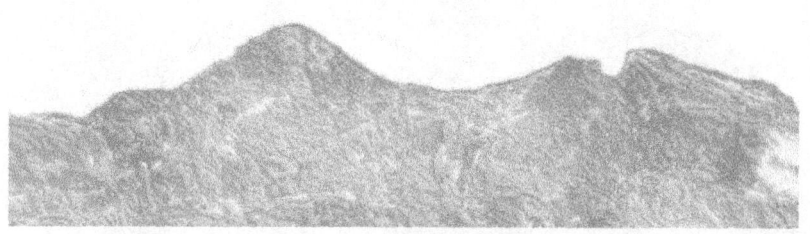

do not ask the wind why it blows
do not ask the tiger why it growls
do not ask the poet why he is drunk

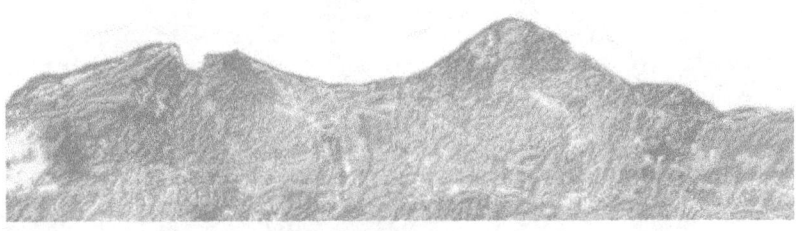

Mountains

a bird flies by
like a feathered stone
the wind wonders

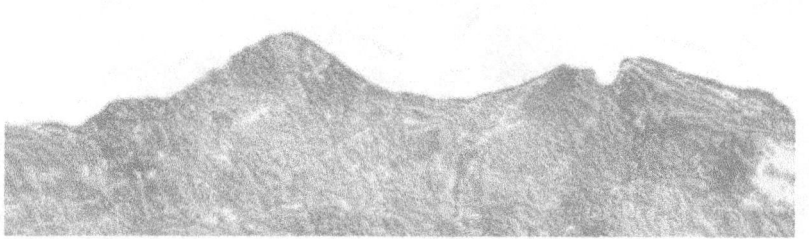

This poet could have been a woman
The mountain and the rain would have been the same
But the wind would have had a different fragrance

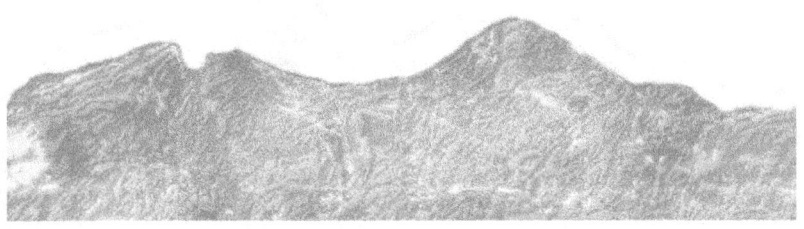

Mountains

the blue sheets are warm
the pillow is fluffy
the summer sky is ready

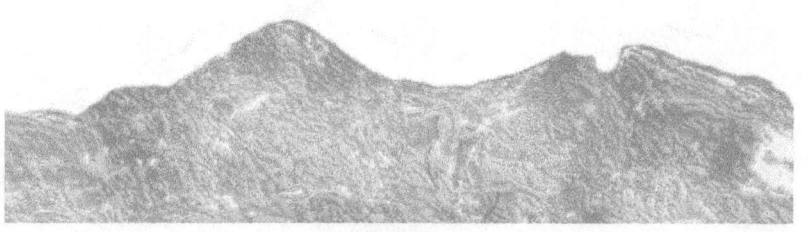

the poet, like the deaf, speaks very well
the poet, like the mute, sees very well,
the poet, like the blind, drinks a lot

Mountains

landscapes are nothing without poets
the poet is nothing without a little dust on his sandals

the poet doesn't care whether he is a man or she is a woman
just drinks the coffee walks the road and sings alone
the rest is only the wind blowing and the distant sound of a
 crazy flute

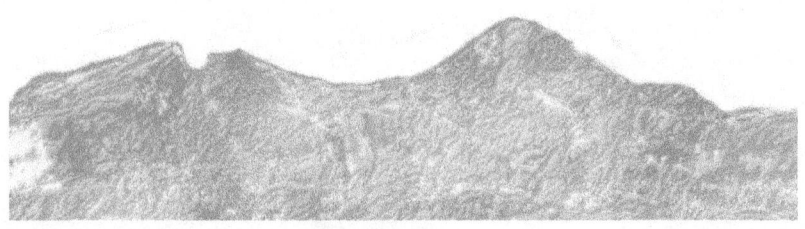

Mountains

darkness falls like in a huge theater
and the poet is irritated
as he can't see the screen
because of the crazy haircuts of the trees

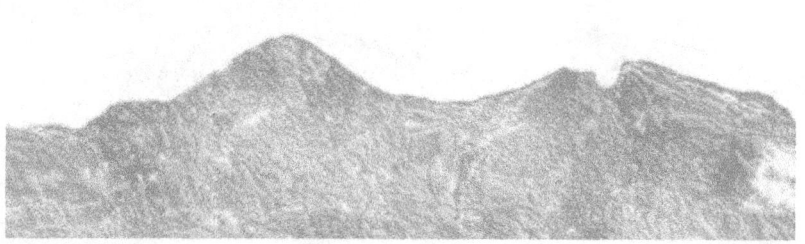

rain types on the roof
like a crazy secretary
—the poet dictates

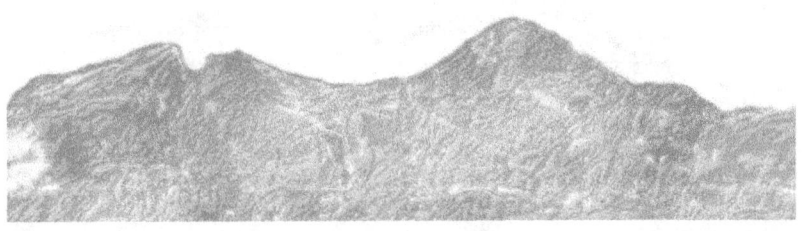

Mountains

this poet is not Japanese
and knows nothing about haikus
this poet writes short poems
because he is a lazy bum

beauty doesn't come from complexity
beauty doesn't come from simplicity
beauty comes from beauty
whatever beauty is

Mountains

"fuck it"
said the poet
he wasn't talking
about poetry
of course

if you say you believe
in only one truth
what are you going to call
the eroding mountain
or the ever changing sea?

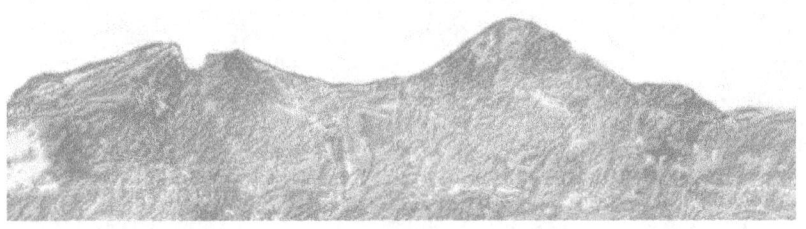

"I can't find you on Facebook!"
the poet complained to poetry
"that's because I only use twitter"
under another name, she thought
but she didn't tell him that

just another poem
about the moon
it deserves it
hanging beautiful
like a gold banana
on a rapper's chest

Mountains

this poet is down down down
"get up!" yells poetry
"and don't forget to pick up
all your mess on the floor!"

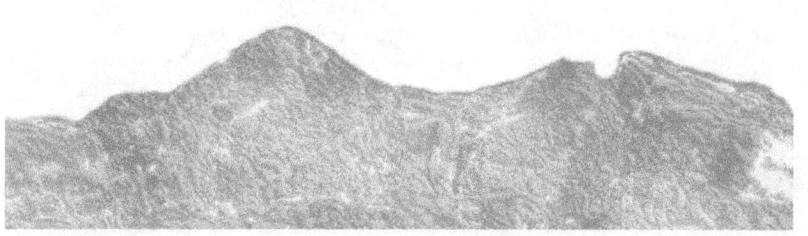

summer
earth sweats
poet sweats
poems melt like ice-cream
only poetry has air conditioning
in her huge empty palace

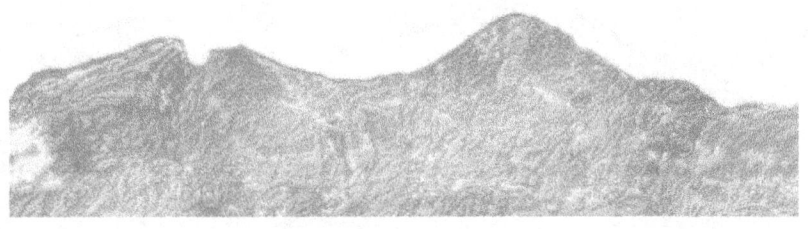

"No one is innocent!" the poet said
"I don't know what you're talking about" poetry retorted
filing her nails and looking glamorous

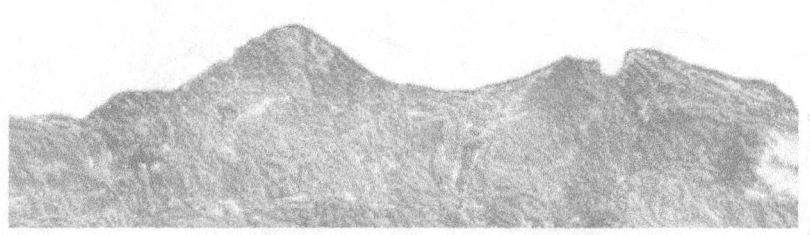

"why write poetry?"
"why not write poetry?"
the poet answers
taking out the garbage
while the first icy star
rises in the warm blue sky

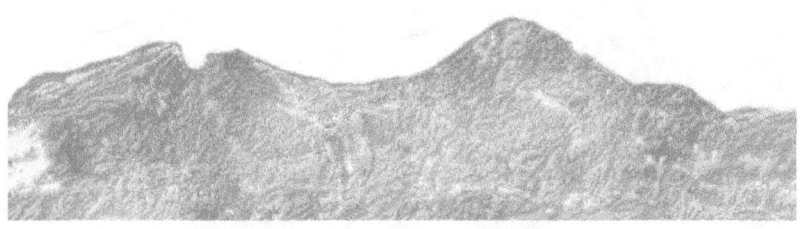

Mountains

"so many deaths"
the poet thinks
the mountain says nothing
the wind says nothing
the bird sings and flies away
the poet writes down the song

ghost voices on the radio
electric winds of memories and sorrow
trying to reach us through the air
but we only listen to the hiss of the boiling water
and the gurgling of our long-awaited cup of coffee

Mountains

"do you think poetry is important for life?"
"No, I think life is important for poetry"
the bird flies from the branch
filling the empty space with the wind
and endless possibilities

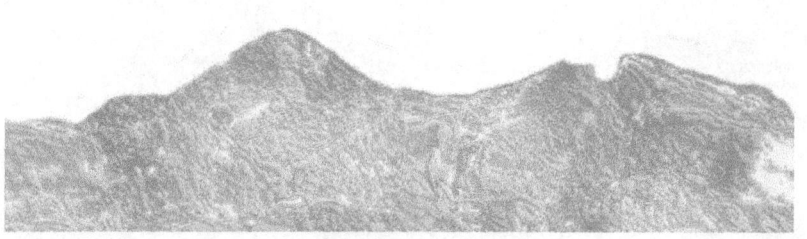

the poet drinks his cold raki
in a little café near Omonia
he knows that "no" has been
what man has said to the gods
when they asked to be worshipped
with expensive sacrifices
and he also knows that poetry
was born on that day
all for man to keep

"who am I?"
the poet asks
"who gives a fuck?"
poetry answers

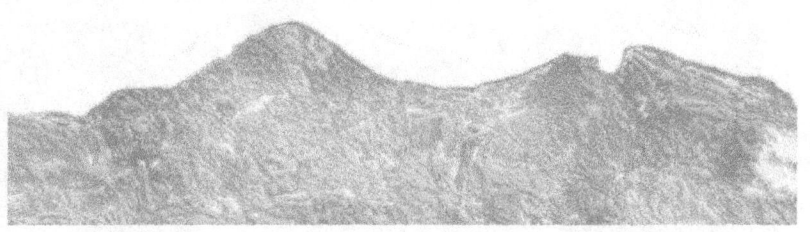

"what is an image?"
"what is the wind?"
"what is a tree?"
"what is a mountain?"
the poet answers
and laughs
lighting a cigarette

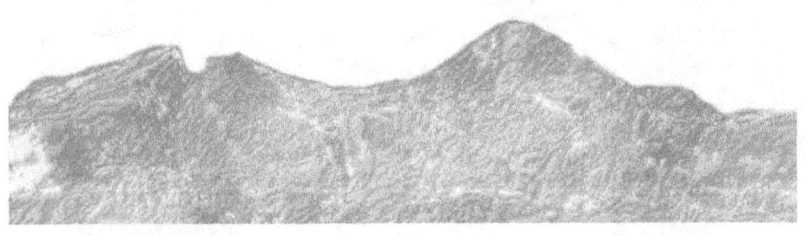

Mountains

the barbarians bang on their shields
while the Greek poet sips his ouzo
and gives the kids a few olives
"ah money," he thinks, "money"
then he looks at the sea
and doesn't think anymore

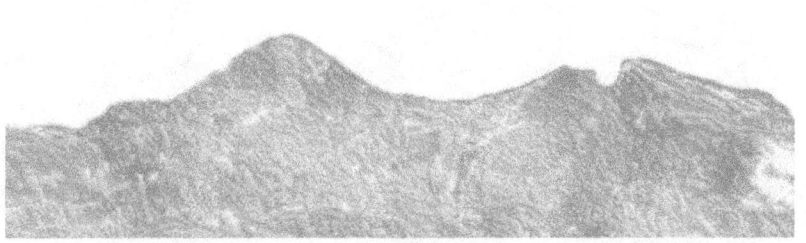

night falls
poet rises
temporary balance

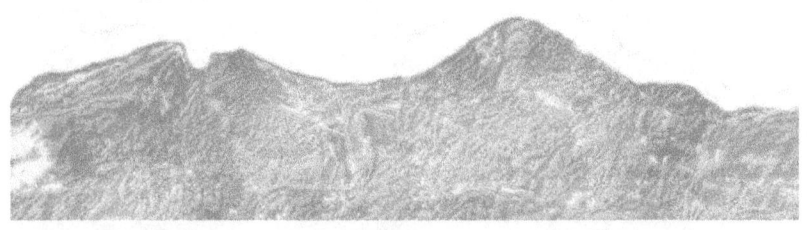

Mountains

the moon fell on the mountain top
and rolled down to the bottom
like a small sliver coin
the poet pocketed it
while nobody was watching

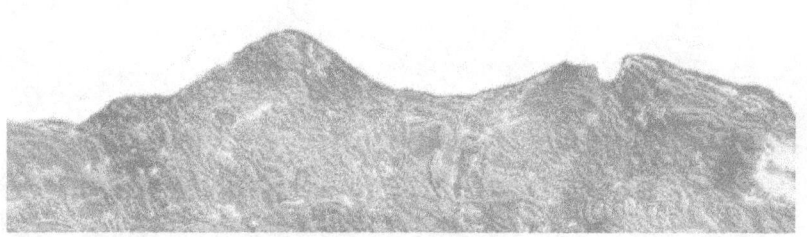

quiet love of the mountains
thunder echo of their hearts
the poet sighs and walks on

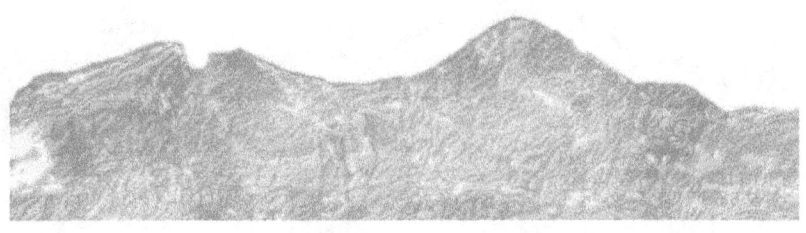

Mountains

the poet takes his hat off
the wind puts it back on

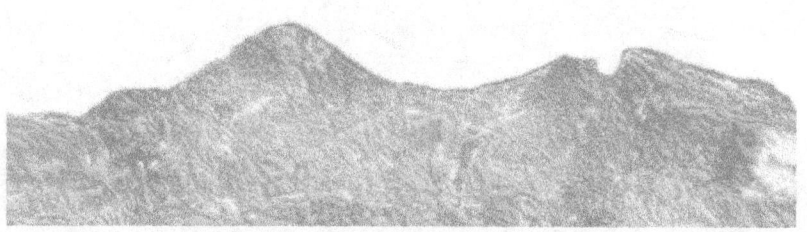

"Ah poetry" the poet sighs
"Ah poets" poetry sighs
not meaning the same thing

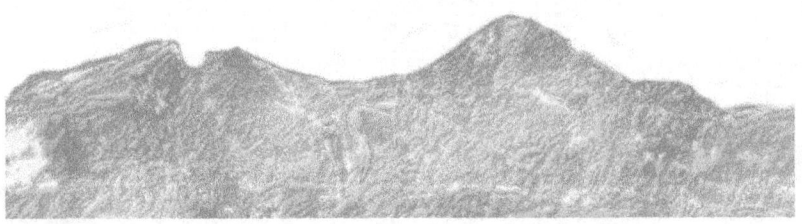

Mountains

this poet wants to be famous
poetry clips a paper crown for him
you can see the tip of her tongue sticking out

this poet is in love with this poet
no words

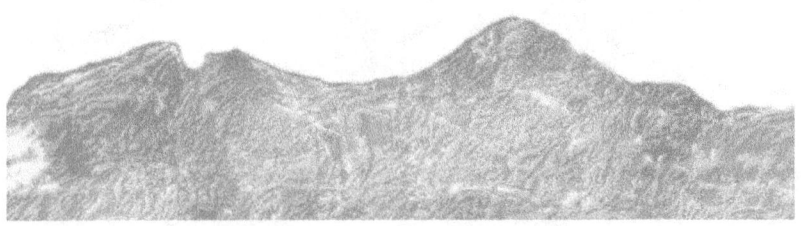

Mountains

night folds her dress
and stretches her dark body
in splendid nakedness
her cold breath blurs
the poet's window
he draws a heart
blows a kiss
and puts an extra log
in the fireplace

"that's it, I quit!" the poet yells
"poetry is quitting" poetry says
"true" the poet says
they go to a café
and talk about the weather

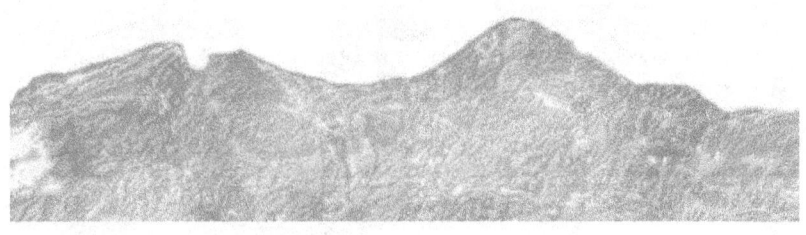

Mountains

"the mountain is a metaphor
for the work of the poet" the poet says
"what mountain?" poetry asks
"exactly" says the poet

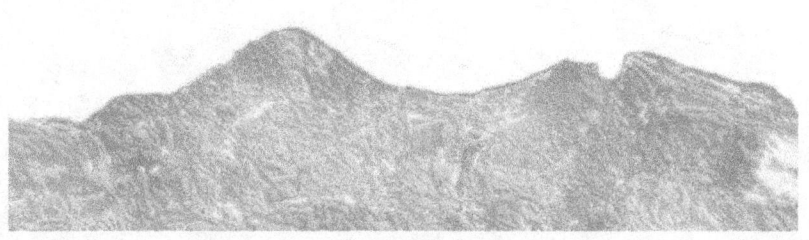

all poems are unfulfilled promises
like the red moon over the trees
and the phone that rings in the empty house

Mountains

this poet thinks about death
poetry puts her hand on his shoulder
it helps

the star falls on the mountain's crown
blinding jewel of dawn

Mountains

the wind blows
the clouds roll
the poet wants to stay home
"go to work" poetry yells
handing him his raincoat

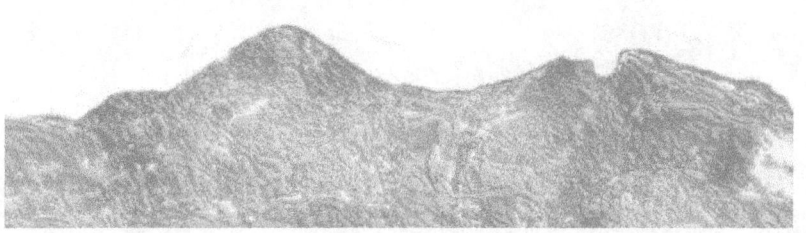

can a poem be only two lines?
no, of course not

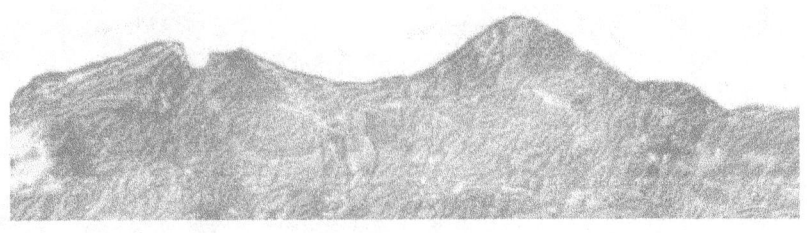

Mountains

the poet takes a selfie
the image is of poor quality

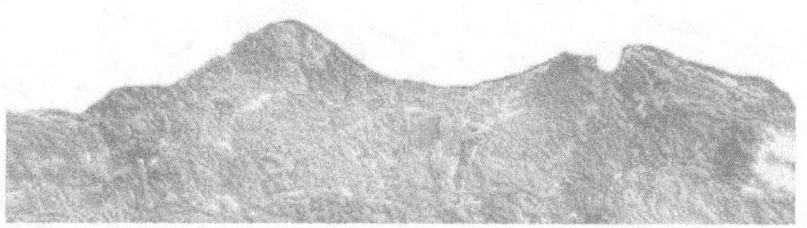

dusk spreads gold dust
on the trees the roofs the cars
the poet sticks out his open hands

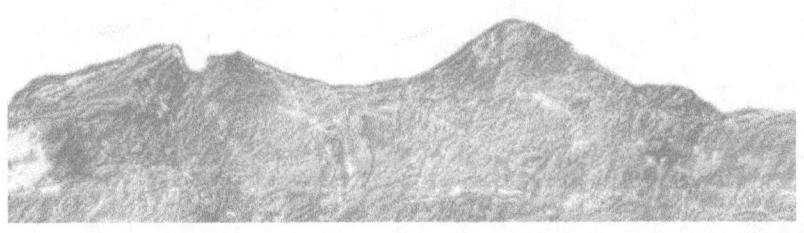

winter's heavy boots
echo in the distance
—the mountains tighten

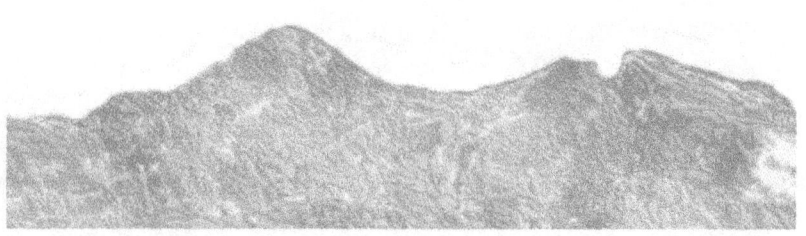

"I want to be a woman" the poet says
"then I'll be your man" poetry replies
the poet has chosen a lovely summer dress
poetry has grown a mustache and sideburns
they look stunning

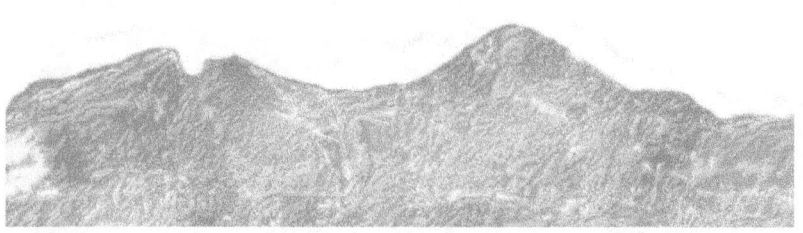

Mountains

the poet writes a verse
smokes a cigarette
drinks a glass of wine
goes for a walk
watches television
calls his mother on the phone
goes to bed
dreams
wakes up
reads the verse
it is terrible
writes another one
"and you wonder why I want a divorce"
poetry says

"am I not the best poet in the world?"
the poet asks
"what world?"
poetry says

Mountains

the car disappears in the curve
the halo of the headlights fade like a whisper
only the road keeps turning in the night

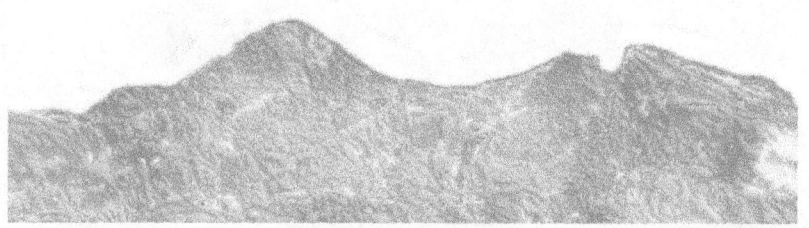

pale sun through the trembling branches
the poet decides it's a sign of hope
while poetry turns the heat up

Mountains

"you're a poet" the kings says
"there are a lot of refugees in my kingdom
write something moving about them"
"you're the king" the poet replies
"do something about them"
the poet is beheaded
and the king shuts
down all the borders

(to Henrik Nordbrandt)

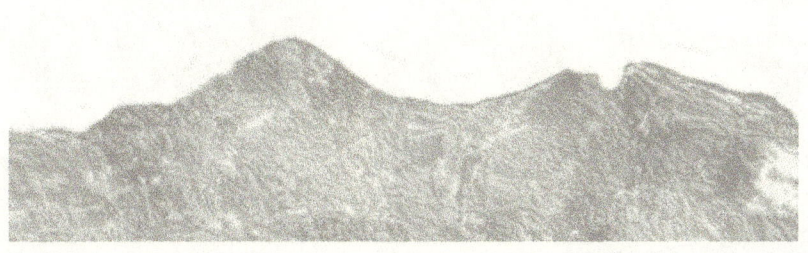

thin silver bow of the disappearing moon
a cloud hangs by like an empty quiver
the poet's heart is pierced by the soft arrow of the night

Mountains

stillness of the fog
the poet procrastinates
blurred images

this poet loves women who smoke
because they don't give a damn
about what other people think
"But I don't smoke" poetry says
The poet remains silent

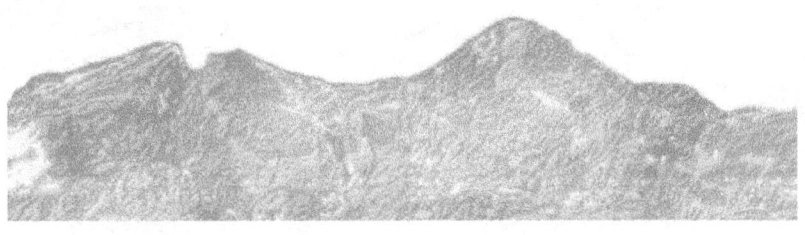

the poet has no inspiration
poetry yawns
the cat yawns
the poet yawns too

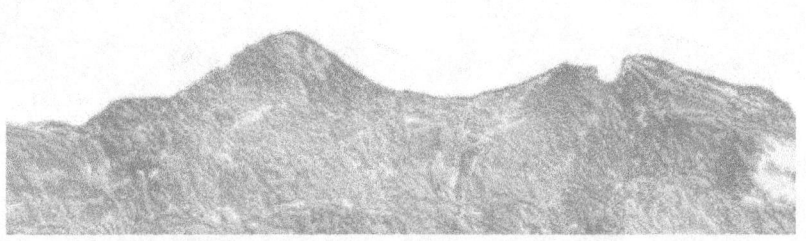

Seb Doubinsky

the trees hide behind the house
wrapped in the fog's see-through veils
nature erotica

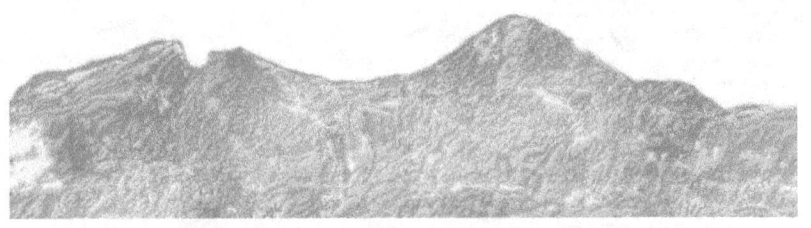

Mountains

this poet wants to be alone
"go away! " he tells poetry
"OK " poetry says and she begins
to gather her things
"No, wait" the poet says

(To Matthew Rohrer)

the poet thinks he has a sad voice
he has a sad voice
but he is the only one to know

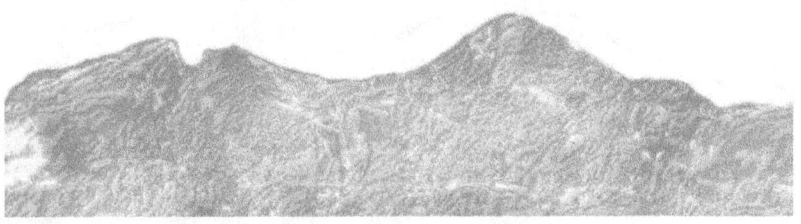

Mountains

this poet finally left her for good
and poetry stares at their empty bed
she never thought she would miss him
but she does
even if it's just a little bit

"I suck!" the poet yells
"all poets suck" poetry answers
"now you're insulting me " the poet says

Mountains

the wind is not red
the wind is not hateful
the wind dries tears
the wind sings
the wind plays
with every one
with everything
the wind doesn't care
but the wind heals
without even knowing why

winter's grip chokes the night
dizzying the moon and stars
the poet puts on his old pullover
and thinks about those who sleep outside
he makes some tea
and thinks about those who sleep outside
he wish he could welcome them all
in his little house
but he cannot
the house is too small
and is too crushed by the night

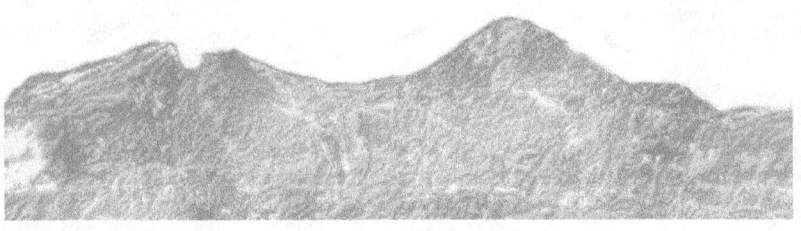

Mountains

the poet thinks about god
then wonders if god thinks about him too
that would be a funny synchronicity
poetry yawns
after the storm we pick up the branches
straighten up the garden chairs
rake the wet grass covered with leaves
after the storm we speak quietly
as the birds are silent still

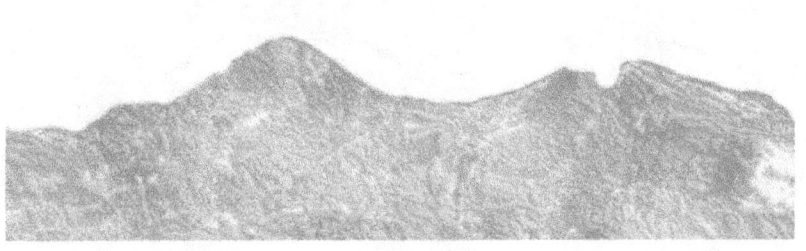

the morning moon
hangs on the blue silk sky
like a thin Buddha smile
the poet bows

Mountains

"did you know that there were more poets in the Résistance
than there were writers or painters?" poetry asks
"that's what constant bullying does to you" the poet says
shadow-boxing in the mirror

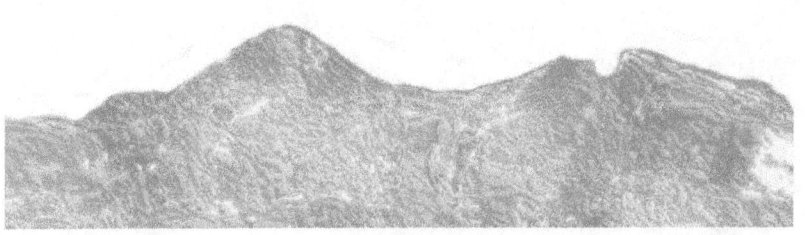

the church bell tolls in the distance
"at least you know it's not for you" poetry says
the poet nods as he lights her cigarette

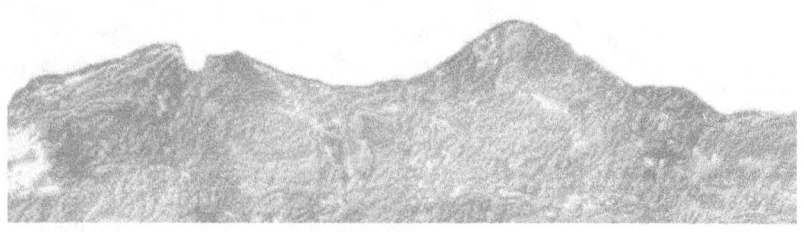

Mountains

they speak about war on the television
the poet waits for his tea to brew
it takes a fucking long time

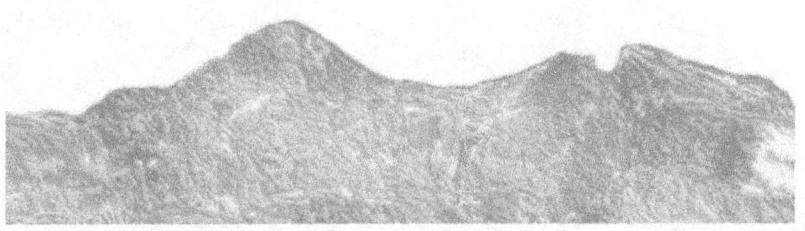

the sun repaints the wall
a temporary gold
the poet thinks he should buy
a lottery ticket

Mountains

the poet looks at his breath
shaping his soul in the freezing morning
then he looks at his blue hands
and rushes home

the poet thinks about the end of the year
how its hair slowly whitened
and how quietly it passed away
"did you remember to put the champagne
In the fridge? " poetry asks
the poet hurries to the kitchen

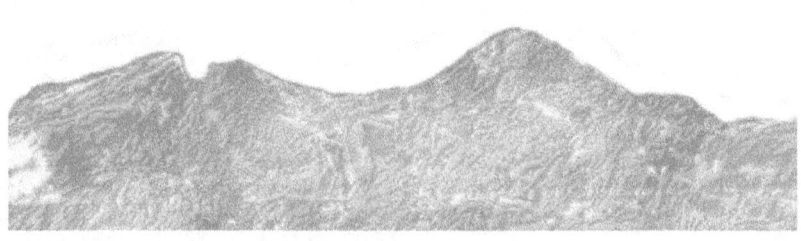

Mountains

the poet looks at a nice parked minivan
"you don't drive" poetry says
they keep walking but the poet looks back twice

(for Justin Grimbol)

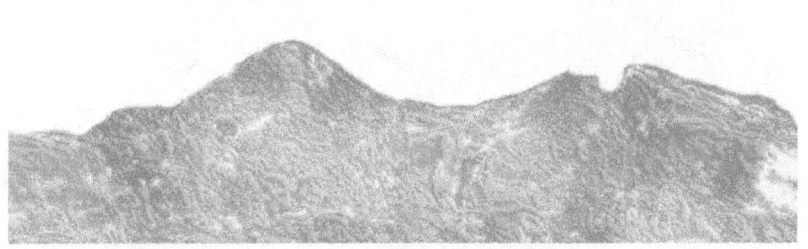

the poet sits down and leans
against the mountain
they both feel warm

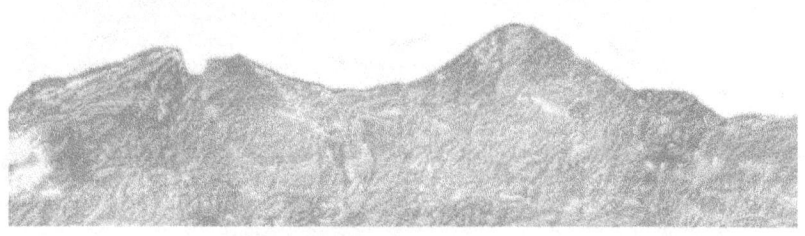

Mountains

the fog lifts like a skirt
over the morning's delicate ankles
victorian winter

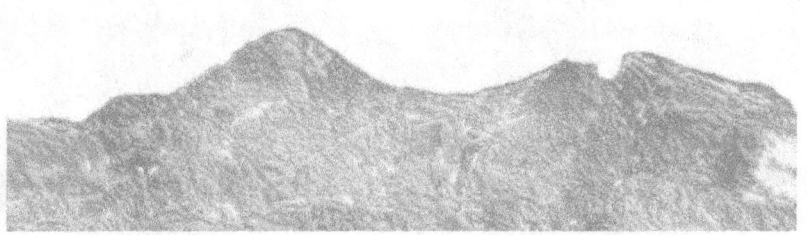

the poet thinks about death
poetry watches TV
night comes home a little drunk
it takes its shoes off not to disturb them

Mountains

night's cold face presses on the window
the poet waves night waves back
old friends don't need words

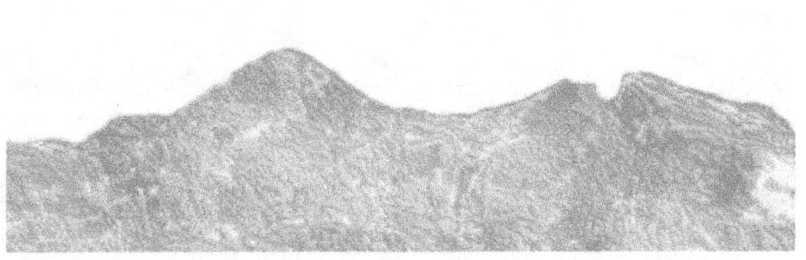

the poet looks through the frozen window
"somebody famous died today" poetry says
a crow lands in front of the house
the poet thinks that the coincidence
would make a terrible poem

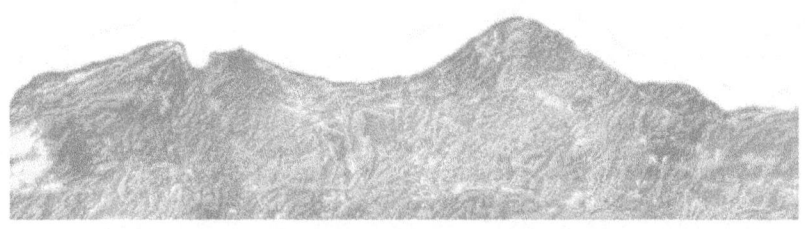

Mountains

"it's been a while since I've written a poem" the poet says
"there you go" poetry says while looking at her crosswords

the poet and the wind are having a conversation
no words

Mountains

the poets writes
poetry watches TV
the cat plays with the night outside
nothing is for certain
except for the pale beauty
of the moon

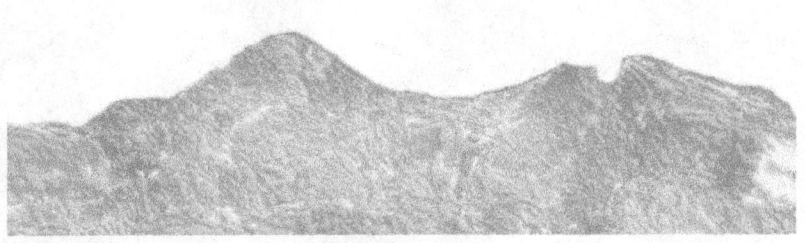

the cat looks at the bird
the bird flies away
the cat looks at the grass

Mountains

rain falls on the mountains
they remain motionless like huge cows
only the poet's hand moves
writing a poem about rain

Seb Doubinsky

the poet hears on the radio
that somebody famous just died
out of his window
the wind plays with the grass
in the spring sunshine
and it looks beautiful

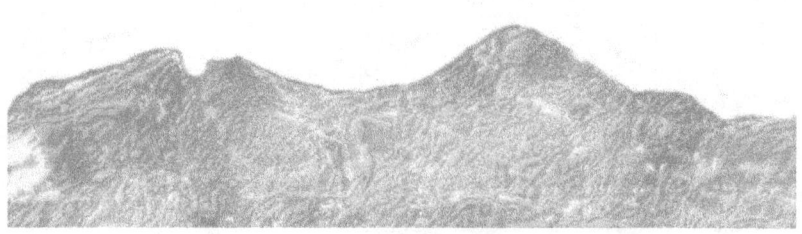

Mountains

what is poetry
without poetry
prose or pure poetry?

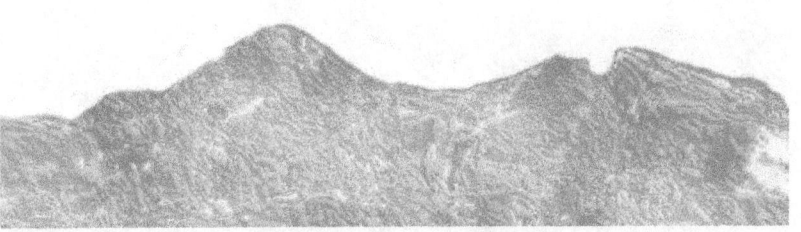

time runs short for the night
thin black thread ready to be cut
by the sun's golden scissors
the poet wonders if he should go to bed
read another page or make himself some stronger coffee

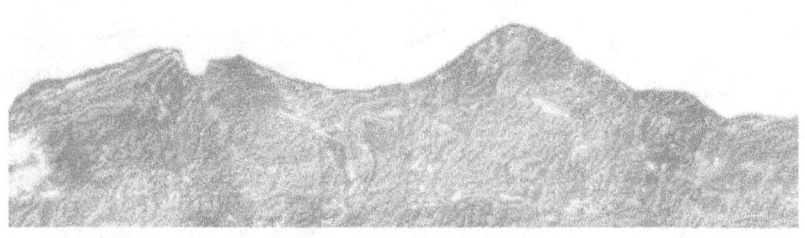

Mountains

"is our love eternal?" the poet asks
"what is love?" poetry asks
"what is eternal?" the house asks

"I want a revolution!" the poet says
"Me too" poetry says "More than anyone else"

Mountains

the bird hops
the cat yawns
the heart fails

the poet picks up
three little white stones on the path
one to remember love
one to remember death
one to give to poetry

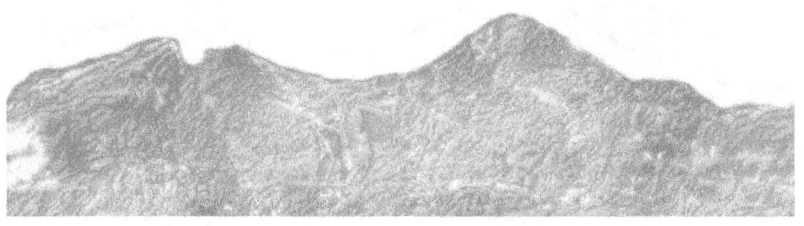

Mountains

a sad song on the radio
the golden powder of dusk
an half-empty bottle of wine
some poems are never meant to be written

the earth turns turns turns very slowly
the poet works works works very slowly
they understand each other perfectly

Mountains

poetry tears the thin sheet of the sky
in long blue ribbons
that disappear as they touch the ground
the poet tries to grab one
but it escapes like cigarette smoke
—ah the lazy sunday afternoons

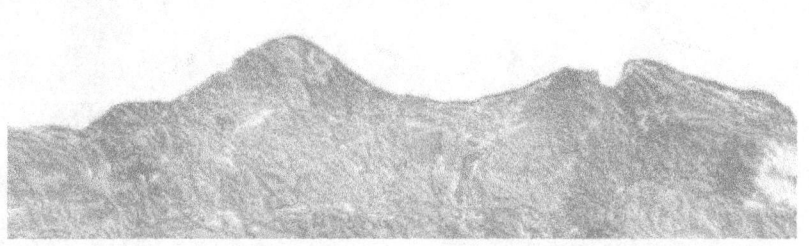

"poetry can change the world!" the poet says
"What's for dinner?" poetry asks

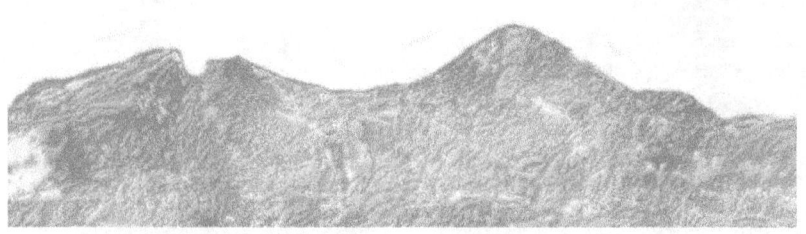

Mountains

the clouds pause to think
over the poet's house
he invites them in for tea

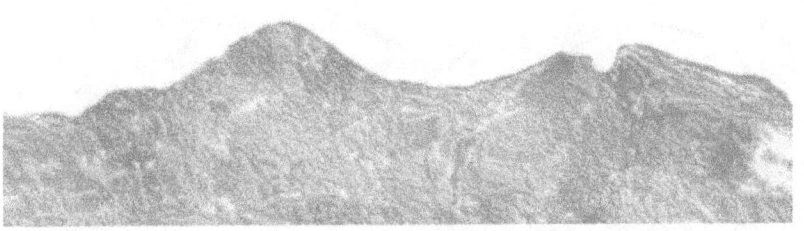

slowly slowly slowly
the stars fall
on the night's blue soil
tiny tiny silver seeds of hope
and unfathomable distances

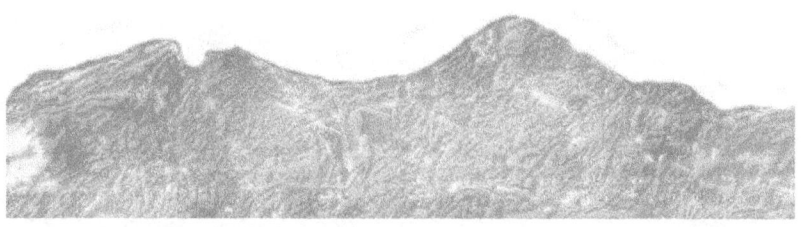

Mountains

the moon caught on a branch
like a beautiful balloon
a child cries

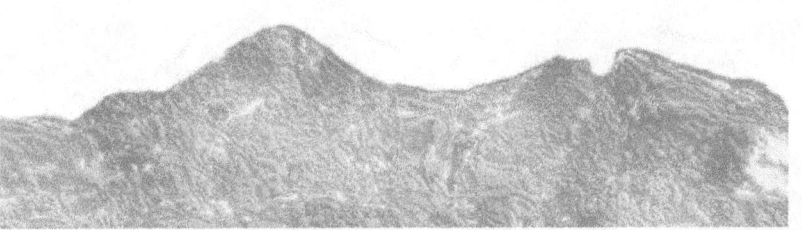

"what is reality?" the poet asks
"everything you don't want it to be" poetry says
refilling his glass of wine

Mountains

what beauty is

a single snowflake falling
from a perfectly blue sky

a tacky plastic souvenir
bought by a child
with its own money

an illusion of harmony
in the indifference of Nature

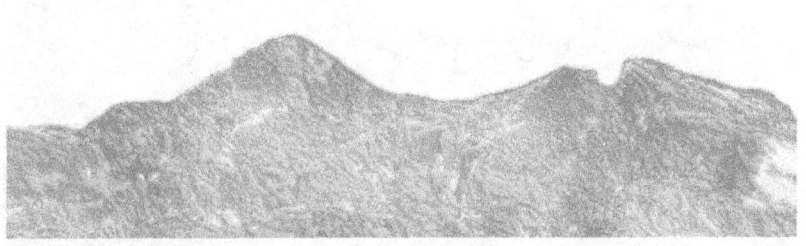

"do you think I am a master?" the poet asks
"a master of what?" poetry says

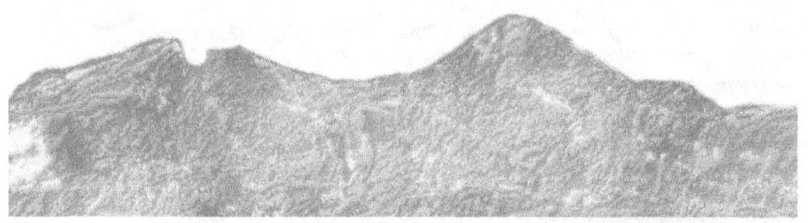

"what is love?" the poet ask
"no idea", poetry says
they both laugh

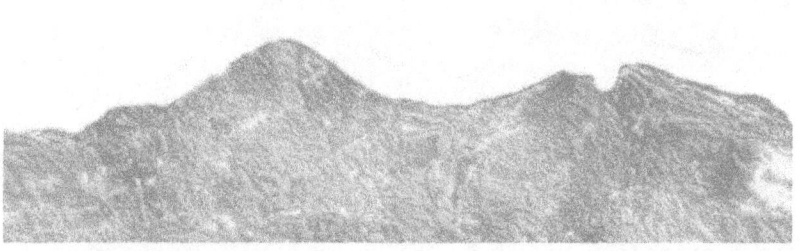

Seb Doubinsky

rocks in the garden
shiny with rain
single tiny monk-ant reaching for the top

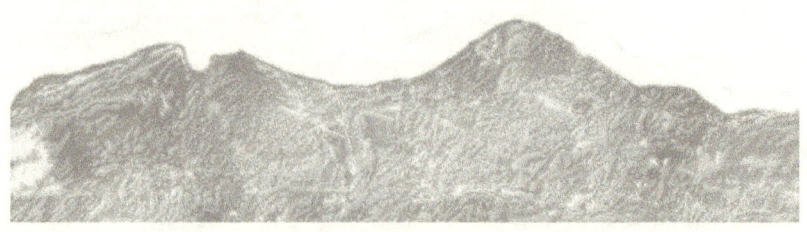

www.ingramcontent.com/pod-product-compliance
Lightning Source LLC
LaVergne TN
LVHW041545070426
835507LV00011B/934